Winner of the L. E. Phillabaum Poetry Award for 2013

Also by Kelly Cherry

POETRY

The Retreats of Thought
Hazard and Prospect: New and Selected Poems
Rising Venus
Death and Transfiguration
God's Loud Hand
Natural Theology
Relativity: A Point of View
Lovers and Agnostics

FICTION

The Woman Who
We Can Still Be Friends
The Society of Friends
My Life and Dr. Joyce Brothers
The Lost Traveller's Dream
In the Wink of an Eye
Augusta Played
Sick and Full of Burning

NONFICTION

Girl in a Library: On Women Writers and the Writing Life
History, Passion, Freedom, Death, and Hope: Prose about Poetry
Writing the World
The Exiled Heart: A Meditative Autobiography

CHAPBOOKS AND LIMITED EDITIONS

Vectors: J. Robert Oppenheimer: The Years before the Bomb (poems)
The Globe and the Brain (essay)
Welsh Table Talk (poems)
An Other Woman (poem)
The Poem (essay)
Time Out of Mind (poems)
Benjamin John (poem)
Songs for a Soviet Composer (poems)
Conversion (story)

TRANSLATIONS

"Antigone," in *Sophocles, 2*
"Octavia," in *Seneca: The Tragedies, Volume II*

The Life and Death of Poetry

POEMS | KELLY CHERRY

LOUISIANA STATE UNIVERSITY PRESS
BATON ROUGE

Published by Louisiana State University Press
Copyright © 2013 by Kelly Cherry
All rights reserved
Manufactured in the United States of America
LSU Press Paperback Original

Designer: Barbara Neely Bourgoyne
Typeface: Whitman

Library of Congress Cataloging-in-Publication Data
Cherry, Kelly.
  The life and death of poetry : poems / Kelly Cherry.
    p. cm.
  "LSU Press Paperback Original."
  ISBN 978-0-8071-5042-9 (pbk. : alk. paper) — ISBN 978-0-8071-5043-6 (pdf) — ISBN 978-0-8071-5044-3 (ePub) — ISBN 978-0-8071-5045-0 (mobi)
  I. Title.
  PS3553.H357L54 2013
  811'.54—dc23

                                                    2012027922

The author wishes to thank the editors and staff of the following publications, in which some of the poems in this book first appeared, sometimes in earlier versions: *Arts and Letters:* "Mute" and "Talking with Only One Functional Vocal Cord"; *Atlantic:* "Field Notes"; *Café Solo:* "A Blue Jay in the Snow"; *Cave Wall:* "The Bright Field," "The First Word," and "The Lizard at Syracuse"; *Christianity and Literature:* "Rain, Early Morning, Bardsey Island"; *Connotation Press, an Online Archive:* "The Loveknot" and "Lovelily"; *Cortland Review:* "Ars Poetica"; *Dominion Review:* "Scene"; *Florida Review:* "Dream Daughter"; *Iron Horse Review:* "Girls" and "The Spring"; *Kenyon Review:* "Learning to Live with Stone"; *Literary Review:* "What the Poet Wishes to Say"; *Literature and Belief:* "A Sunday in Scotland"; *New South:* "Frontward"; *New Welsh Review:* "On Bardsey Island" and "Men Who Go to Work Each Day"; *Per Contra:* "Night Vowels"; *Poemelon:* "Wintering" and "Against Aphasia"; *Southern Poetry Review:* "Which Is a Verb"; *Vineyards:* "Seen but Not Heard."

"The Conversation" first appeared in *Mothers and Daughters*, edited by June Cotner (New York: Harmony Books, 2001). "Welsh Song" was reprinted in *When She Named Fire: An Anthology of Contemporary Poetry by American Women*, edited by Andrea Hollander Budy (Pittsburgh: Autumn House Press, 2008). "The Bright Field" was reprinted in *Entering the Real World: VCCA Poets on Mt. San Angelo*, edited by Margaret B. Ingraham and Andrea Carter Brown (Amherst, Va.: Wavertree Press, 2011). "What the Poet Wishes to Say" was republished in *Read More*, a newsletter associated with the *Literary Review*.

Sixteen of the eighteen poems in "Welsh Table Talk" were published in a fine limited edition under that title, sponsored by the College of Liberal Arts of the University of Alabama at Huntsville and with art by Michael Crouse (Washington, D.C.: Book Arts Conservancy, 2004). The author is deeply indebted to the college, the publisher, Michael Crouse, and designers John Paul Greenawalt and Stephen L. Vanilio for that gorgeous volume.

The paper in this book meets the guidelines for permanence and durability of the Committee on Production Guidelines for Book Longevity of the Council on Library Resources. ∞

For my students, then and now

Man makes the word, and the word means nothing which the man has not made it mean, and that only to some man. But since man can think only by means of words or other external symbols, these might turn round and say: "You mean nothing which we have not taught you, and then only so far as you address some word as the interpretant of your thought." In fact, therefore, men and words reciprocally educate each other. . . . Thus my language is the sum total of myself; for the man is the thought.

—C. S. Peirce, "Some Consequences of Four Incapacities," 1868

Ontology recapitulates philology.

—Old joke

Contents

LEARNING THE LANGUAGE

Which Is a Verb 3
A Sunday in Scotland 4
Fields with Shrew 5
   The Bright Field 5
   Field Notes 6
Seen but Not Heard 7
A Blue Jay in the Snow 8
The Loveknot 9
Night Vowels 10
The First Word 11
Learning the Language 12
Mute 14
Frontward 15
Talking with Only One Functional Vocal Cord 16
Against Aphasia 17
Language 19
The Lizard at Syracuse 20
Wintering 21
Fiction 23
Chekhov in Yalta 24
"Lovelily" 25
Poetic Justice 26
Ars Poetica 28
Underwriting the Words 29
A Voice Survives 31

WELSH TABLE TALK (A SEQUENCE)

Welsh Song 35

On Bardsey Island 36

Rain, Early Morning, Bardsey Island 37

The Mad Friar 38

The Sheep-Fly 39

Scene 40

Welsh Table Talk 41

Line Fishing 42

The Conversation 43

Dream Daughter 44

Girls 46

A Woman in Wales 47

The Spring 48

Men Who Go to Work Each Day 49

A Day Spent Walking and Writing 50

The Manx Shearwater 51

The Last Night 52

Learning to Live with Stone 53

WHAT THE POET WISHES TO SAY

On Translation 57

What the Poet Wishes to Say 62

The Life and Death of Poetry 66

Learning the Language

Which Is a Verb

We fell out of eternity
into time, which is a verb.
Life was rushing past us,
and we began to rush too.
Everything was a blur. In the confusion,
some things got mixed up with others.
A loaf of bread drove a bus.
A longleaf pine swam in the pond.

We grew so dizzy, light sparked
beneath our closed eyelids, like rescue flares.
We lay down on the red grass
and clung to the world as it whirled.

Wind whistled past our ears.
Tears flew from our eyes.

A Sunday in Scotland

I found a path that led me through the wood,
past fallen stone—a Roman wall in ruin—
and some felled trees, to where two horses stood
at pasture, and the nearest, a graceful roan,
drew close, and backed away again, and then
came partway back, and then decided to get on
with his own life in that field next to a fen.
I found a stump nearby—something to sit on
while catching my breath. Just to my right, a field
of poppies, post-impressionistically
spattered. The sky was gray. The church bells pealed,
and I was thinking how it would be, to be
on earth as horse or dog or cat or bird
or tree or flower, self-consciousness deferred.

Fields with Shrew

The Bright Field

Face sharp and narrow as a pencil,
the shrew is a graffito
in the bright field

Nature is a book,
it has been said,
and perhaps God is its author,
and perhaps not

but every living thing
inscribes itself on land, sea, or air
Even rock, even sun
make a statement

Here, we say, *here*
And we say, *There you are*
and there you are

Field Notes

Death underfoot wherever you walk,
overhead, at hand.

The bird flat on its back,
the shrew, its face sharp as a pencil.

And the bee silent upon the sill.

The spider whose web goes on snagging flies for dinner
even after she's been bagged and eaten.

A shrew is so small,
it is amazing that it lives at all,

with a tail as long as a tirade.

Seen but Not Heard

A thrill of cobwebs in the trees,
the breeze strumming gossamer like a guitar.
What's to be done about these bright notes,
this unuttered air?

There must be a melody
heard only by the bees
and flies who die
to hear its harmonies,

a melody like none other,
accomplished and uncanny.
O these night notes,
these undertones, these useless prayers

no human hears.

Night returns to day.
Cobwebs tremble in lighted air.
Beeches catch the sun
and toss it back like a ball,

and trapped things pray
sotto voce.

A Blue Jay in the Snow

A blue jay in the snow
is a text
that cannot be read
out of the context
of the snow falling
around us,
a widening margin
everywhere,
until we are stranded
in the middle of the page,

which seems, now, to be written
in a foreign language
that we do not know,
cannot read,
the margin the blank
undifferentiated whiteness
into which
the blues of the articulated world
bleed.

Note: Blues are—or were—a stage in the process of book publication; for the most part, they have been replaced by digital proofs. The type and illustrations in blues were blue; the production editor used them for a final review of various major details. They were particularly useful for checking the relationship of illustration to text in children's books, as in determining whether an illustration would bleed into the margins or gutter.

The Loveknot

On the couch—
baby mice stillborn,
would-be twins
clutching each other
as if either
could save his brother.

The size of thumbs,
tails still curled.

Two Q's
spelling nothing.

Spelling it twice.

Night Vowels

Breath of wind that clouds the moon.
Shriek of eagle, cry of loon

threading through fog.
The throaty frog.

Death-scream of a mouse
the roaming cat returns with and proffers on the stoop.

And is that you I hear, weeping
while the rest are sleeping?

O, O, O, O, O
u, u, u.

The First Word

Someone said it. Maybe
a child calling for his mother.
Maybe a lover, inventing
the word *you*. Maybe
a hunter giving his clan
the signal to kill.

Was there delight on the mother's face?
Did the beloved preen in the mirror of her lover?
And the beast, alarmed
by the human swarm
around him—did he hear
the tribesman's command
and know that it was the last word?

Learning the Language

Alex, African grey parrot, 1976–2007

Before he had the word for it
he must have apprehended the thing itself:
its raptures, obligations,
that it supported his right to exist.

He knew the cool warmth
of her unfeathered skin
beneath his claws, saw
how she smiled broadly when
his wings grazed her bare arm,
his black bill nudged her hand
resting on the arm of the chair,
he flew from his perch to her nape.

Or did he put on knowledge
with her caress, her constant coo
and call?
        She gave him
a lexicon for life in the lab
a way to speak his world
and if *love* was a word
it had to mean
something, meant what mattered most.

And so he responded, convinced
by her mouth and human throat
shaping sound: *red, green, yellow,*
more, none, same, different, other, banana, kiss.

He had thought they were singing a duet
and that they would go on singing forever.
Good night, he told her, that last night.
I love you, he said.
See you in the morning.

Mute

Perplexity had struck me dumb.
        To say anything would be to attract attention,
which I didn't want.
        The darkening sky murmured
rain, clouds scowling like grownups.
        A dark red throw lay on the couch
as if recovering from a cold.

My mother was strong
        except when she disintegrated
into hysteria.
        My father tore up her picture,
but he had copies. I hope he didn't drown
        the helpless kittens (Wynken,
Blynken, and Nod).

The trees were passing secrets to one another,
        we could hear them whispering.
The TV complained about everything.
        To say *anything*
would have been to exhaust myself
        with rage.
Better to be silent,

to hold one's peace
        as though it were something
a child could carry around
        like a Raggedy Ann,
faded, floppy,
        but consoling,
quiet as a library.

Frontward

My redheaded brother learned the alphabet backward
before he got it right,
because our father read it backward
off the child's blackboard
behind my brother's back.

My restless sister taught herself to speak backward
because she was bored on the school bus.
The signs she saw no one else saw.
No one understood her.
My husband would have; he did that too.

I say the alphabet frontward
and I speak frontward.
I love the way a frontward language
spills into the future, the river into its mouth.

Talking with Only One Functional Vocal Cord

It's work to push the syllables out,
and sometimes they stick inside
like children refusing to go outside
to play, and then I have to shout

though what comes out is a whisper,
a kid too shy to make friends
on the playground, who pretends
to like being alone. I have a sister

who played the flute at Wigmore Hall,
her fingering fluent as a goldfinch in flight.
I think of her late at night
when speech stops and the silenced call.

Against Aphasia

1

The words have flown
sprouted wings and taken off

Your throat is an empty nest

Come back, you want to cry,
but you can't—

You learn to write.
It's the only way.

2

One day birds line up
on a branch of the cedar

to take their turns at the feeder.

You name them chickadee, bunting, wren—

words you can't say
but still believe in

3

So you write
and words line up on the ruled page
like birds on a branch
and sing to you

the sparrow his spunk
the robin, matins
the bluebird his happiness

You feel like crowing.

Language

Conceals and discloses.
Lies and belies.
Discourses on roses
("A rose is a rose is . . .").
May be a disguise.

May invoke a muse.
Or obfuscate.
You choose:
Purple prose?
Boilerplate?

Language is a sorcerer
and may so entrance
the dedicated listener
she cannot tell the dancer from the dance
or syntax from the sense.

And it may ennoble
the soul, electrify the mind,
beautify the Chernobyls
of our devastated hearts, and enable
us to know our human kind.

The Lizard at Syracuse

A small, slim lizard
slipped swiftly as light
into a crevice of
the wall of
the crumbling Greek theater.

Lizard, I thought,
your ancestors attended
the tragedies of Aeschylus.

You yourself
may have seen the clouds on Mount Etna,
or the human comedy.

Miniature shooting star,
cold-blooded Perseid in the bleachers,
you are the exemplar of a plot
that heeds not the unity of time.

Do you find the comedy raucous,
blue, and desperate? Does it need polish, sparkle?
A sense of irony?

Well then, you are the irony.
The greatest irony in the world.

Are we laughing yet?

Wintering

The asparagus, the ivy, and the anonymous
summer vines, unleafed, snarled in snow,
lean against the wire dog-pen.
The wind is from River Falls,
and before that, Idaho. My house is lighted
against the dark. On their shelves, books

huddle in their jackets. I have read the books
that tell of difficult journeys and anonymous
desires, of lanterns that have lighted
the way to Arcadia or the North Pole, books that explain snow,
or the way living things grow, or the way lovers fall
in love, each to the other an open

book, as if love were the pen
writing, and their lives a book.
I stand looking out as the snow falls
obsessively. The night is anonymous.
Supper will be snow
baked in the oven I have lighted,

birch bark, roots, and berries, dressed with light,
served on a paper plate with a pen
for a fork—a low-calorie diet, light as a single snow-
flake, not found in cookbooks
but typical of anonymous
readers en route from Wisconsin to Borneo or Victoria Falls.

While I eat, I read and the snow falls
on the tangled vines too light-
weight to stand up to snow. Anonymous

as a nun, I write books, pushing my pen
across paper, or read others' books,
in a room as quiet as falling snow.

It's no
secret that one who reads can occasionally fall
to thinking how life in books
is so much more exciting and enlightening
than her real life, in which she's penned
up, isolate, and anonymous.

*The snow falls
lightly as starlight* is the sort of thing one reads in books
penned by Anon.

Fiction

It has a plot,
or, fashionably, not.

Characters live
and die, mostly
the ones we love.

The setting
is where the characters live
and die. A modern executive
does not often live or die
in rural Mississippi.

In a novel, dialogue need not be so concise
as in a short story and may continue
for hundreds of pages,
which we will turn if what is said
is interesting enough.

Is Monsieur short and squat?
Does Madame wear a hat?
Would Mademoiselle enjoy
a ladyfinger?

There may be symbols, too.
That ladyfinger *means* something.

At last the theme
reveals itself, taking
it all off under the hot lights,
the cool gaze,
the critical view.

Chekhov in Yalta

Rain darkening the red squares of terraces,
      the gray stones of walkways.

Crows on a cable. And seagulls. (Of course.)

Imagine Chekhov tending to his roses,
      talking to them, teasing and encouraging them.

Imagine the roses, their coy fluttering
      on the stalk as he approaches.

And after he goes back into the house,
      what they say among themselves.

Their rustling skirts, the susurrant sighs.
      Black Sea blue against blue skies.

Him at his desk, jacket off,
      proceeding to revise.

"Lovelily"

Adverb. With which Virginia Woolf describes
the flight-fatigued birds, how they "came descending,
delicately declining, dropped down and
sat silent on the tree"—an elm grown tall—
and on a wall. . . . Or is the word a typo?
But never mind, for does it not call forth
whole acres of lovely lilies in bloom, a kind
we'll call love lilies, stems and petals swayed
by breezes, like a woman's blowing skirt
or like her hair when, after love, she rises
from the bed and glances in the mirror
to see what changes have been worked on her,
and isn't she changed, become somebody else,
more knowing, more aware of who she is?

Poetic Justice

> The quality of mercy is not strain'd.
> It droppeth like the gentle rain from heaven.
> —*The Merchant of Venice*, Act 4, Scene 1

Not from the poet—
from somewhere—where?—
the poem acquires

the quality of mercy,

reviving us
as does the gentle rain
green leaves;

it is not strain'd

but touches us all,
a miracle
like the loaves and fish,

that democratic dish.

In dark times,
when the city is discouraged
by its own malfeasance

or difficult circumstance,

the poem instructs us
in responsibility.
When we are alone

and abject or anxious,

hiking a little-known trail
through hieroglyphic woods,
the signs impossible to read

by starlight,

the poem assures us
we are forgiven,
we are but

human.

Ars Poetica

No dog, the muse cannot be leashed or trained.
The poem depends upon a *willing* muse.
Nothing is guaranteed or foreordained.

The poem is providential—a blessing gained
in bars and bordellos as often as in pews.
The poet knows the poem is not ordained.

Words upon a page are barely restrained
by form, twist like dust devils to get loose.
Nothing is guaranteed or foreordained.

Like the four winds, words will not be chained
down in stanzas merely to amuse.
The poet knows the poem is not ordained.

Even your life is not your own, feigned
as it is to please the gods—a futile ruse.
Nothing is guaranteed or foreordained.

From time to time, the mercurial muse has deigned
to breathe a poem for a poet's temporary use.
No faithful dog, the muse—nor leashed nor trained.
Nothing's guaranteed. Nothing's foreordained.

Underwriting the Words

Ousted from heaven,
we crashed to language.
Incomparable music
gave way to words.
Authors filled auditoriums
with their friends.
Orpheus wrote a novel.

Some days we try to climb back.
We search for the word that sings,
the sentence that sings.
It's not the same.
Remember the music?
It lifted you up to the light
and endowed you with understanding.

None of us understands anymore.
Commentators baffle, words
reinvent their meaning, every voice
contradicts another. In a city
of deserted streets, where people hide
like turtles, in their houses,
silence is the one common denominator.

The hidden theme of books is silence.
Between the lines,
underwriting the words:
silence.
In every line, we read
the absence of perfect sound,
the severed head with mouth sewn shut.

The hidden theme of books is our obliteration:
that we are swept away
like fallen leaves from the front steps,
insect shells from a sill,
drafts from a desk.

A Voice Survives

for George Garrett (1929–2008)

Sometimes a voice survives
to be heard among the devastation,
the windy ruins of Babel,
the loud trash we make of our lives.

This voice returns us to sense,
delights and engages,
marries us to language.

Excavates the beauty of circumstance.

This voice reveals us to ourselves,
opens the dead-bolt door, lights
the dim passageway all the way
to the store room, with its dust-besotted shelves

stocked with what we thought we had dismissed—
the traveling circus, the woman on the subway,
the soldier with his scarred face, the small boy
at bat in late afternoon, the fly ball kissed

by sunlight—it all comes back
borne on a single voice
calling us out of chaos
to the world before babble and yak.

Welsh Table Talk

(A Sequence)

Welsh Song

Rain blew against the window pane.
The kestrel's shadow quartered the air.
A rooster crowed. The drainpipe banged
Against stone. The child brushed her hair

And sang a song. The gas fire burned.
The gas lamp glowed. The rain fell faster.
Blue became black in the window.
The wind pulled the sea up to the pasture.

The child brushed her hair and sang songs.
The lost pigeon sheltered alone
In the chapel rafters. The red
Glass on the sill gleamed in gaslight.

A winged darkness crossed the dark night,
And the drainpipe banged against stone.

On Bardsey Island

An island of wild wheat and long grass,
The whitewashed abbey at the foot of the mountain,
And the chough, here as if to report
Gloucester has been blinded—
That old news from the mainland.

And wind from the north shrieking its own sad cries.

The Connemara mares switch their tails,
Lift their heads to smell the wind.

Children are playing cards
On the living room floor,
And the door has swung open.

At night, the ghosts of eremites
Flicker in the mist,
Slip quickly as swifts
Through the silent abbey
Along unlighted garden paths,
Among secret coves with shallow water
And high caves.

Rain, Early Morning, Bardsey Island

The Irish Sea, secreted in mist,
Rain falling on the stone
Cottage.

No sun.
Only a silver-plated sky,
The gulls crying.

Fat sheep, invisible in fog, lying
Down, the rams with gold, sprung
Horns like flames,

As if burning,
Sacrificed to
A human yearning.

And monks who lived here
Among sea-slick rocks, on fire
With cold ideas of damnation

And penitence,
Return, almost real,
Almost incarnate,

Almost articulated
In flesh and word.

The Mad Friar

The friar has gone mad.
He dances in the tower
Of the fallen ancient abbey
By candlelight in bright
Day, and a flashing wind
Lifts his gray hair
And gray beard like waves
Breaking offshore.
He dances without music
Unless he hears a music
None else hears
And his rough brown habit
Swirls around his shoes
And the sleeves spread wide
On the wind like wings,
And the rope around his waist
Is the noose he'll hang from.

The Sheep-Fly

You poured that very expensive
Wine, recommended, you assured us, by your vintner,
Into small kitchen glasses, making a toast.
Though evening had come ashore,
The sun was taking a long time
To set; we had already eaten.
You handed glasses to the girls, too,
Who gulped, and moved outside to play.
When I glanced again at my glass
I saw that a sheep-fly had fallen
In. How it struggled, the thin legs
Paddling, wings fluttering in white wine
As if they would be water wings.
I waited for you to offer me another glass.
Or better—more romantic—to swap
Your glass for mine. Instead,
You said, Will you allow me to get that out
For you, and reached in and cupped the now-
Dead fly in your fist.
I was expected to finish my wine, then, and you
Were annoyed with me when the best I could do
Was a few more half-hearted sips.
I had failed your test.
All kinds of possibilities were dying like flies.

Scene

The curtain flies in the open window.
The girls are jumping on and off
The bed on which their father slept.
He has gone out in anorak
And wide-brimmed hat and Wellingtons,
And with a walking stick. The girls
Pretend that one of them is sick.
The curtain falls still, so still its shadow
Seems painted on the windowsill.
The toy penguin on the table
Has its wings spread wide. The girls
Play school and mark each other's papers.
(They have grown tired of smelling-salts,
The vapors.) He has reached the top
Of the mountain (for I can see
Him from here). The curtain stirs,
Snags on thorns and burs. The girls
Play war and snip out pics of ships
And Spam. On an island like this,
Lacking reference points, everything
At a distance looks huge, and seen
From the crown of the furze-covered mountain,
A rooster will look as big as a man.
The girls bring tea to the toy penguin.
The freed curtain flies in the open
Window, and the jam-jar daisies
That were picked from the garden spill
On the floor like girls galore.

Welsh Table Talk

There is a dragon in the garden,
The first one says. Papá, says the second,
Seated cheerfully on the rescued church pew,
Bronwen has put her cold mittens

To my leg. The dragon in the garden
Is quite a nice dragon, says Papá.
The second one says, Nasty Bronwen
Has put her cold mittens to my ears.

The first one says, The dragon is eating
All the mulberries, and the roses
As well. Papá shakes his bald head
And says, I never cared for roses

Myself. The second one squeals, Bronwen,
Stop it! The first one says, The dragon
Is eating the garden and there won't be any
Garden left. Papá likes Marmite

And margarine on his toast, and seventeen
Cups of tea a day. The first one says,
How sad it is that our garden is gone.
The second asks Bronwen to come out and play.

Line Fishing

Papá and daughter fish in shape-shifting pools
That lurk among the sheared-off rocks.
Their lines play out from hand-held spools.
But then: "I'm bored," she says and breaks

For freedom. Oh Gwynnie's gone
To look for her young friend,
The golden doe-eyed fawn
Named Bronwen.

Papá and I avoid each other's gaze:
He's focusing on fish.

Before the sun's burned off the morning haze
We've thought each other selfish.

The voices of the girls carry from the chapel
A cappella.

The Conversation

She has found a snail
And lets it travel her arm.
Look, she says. Isn't it sweet?

(I think she is sweet,
Wonder if she's my stepdaughter-to-be.)

The eyes sentinel atop two small stalks
Like periscopes.

Its face is blank as wax,
Translucent, the shell
A sand-and-cream swirl,
A kind of mint.

She waits patiently
While the snail traverses her arm,

Which is brown with summer,
Smooth as a snail's shell.

We have so far to go.
We have come this far.

Dream Daughter

I heard you singing
In the chapel,
Pedaling the tired piano,

Crashing chords with abandon.
I saw you washing your hair
In holy water,

Saw you braiding your hair
As you walked on the mountainside,
Wind gently slapping the thrift

Back and forth,
Fennel and thyme
Sheltering beneath blue mallow.

Your hair, sun-dried and set
Loose, tumbled and fanned
Out in waves. The sea waved back.

The white duck with red markings
Around its eyes
Rolled from side to side like a sailor

As it crossed the grass.
Later, in the garden,
Where the mallow was,

By moonlight
I saw you setting tea-things on a table,
And the wind snapped the tea towel

Smartly, and the brass
Kettle you were holding by the handle
Shone, a star.

Girls

They go off somewhere
Where they can't be found,
And there they paint the sun
In watercolor, write
Poems about horses.

Or else they sit stubbornly in rain,
A plastic sheet over their heads,
Wanting to know how it feels to be homeless.

Wildflowers and flowering weeds blossom in their hair,
Bracelet small wrists.

There is such a power here,
It could turn the earth on its axis.

The shy, smiling girl.
The bold girl in blue jeans who twists on the couch,
Crossed legs over her head—
She rolls her eyes,
Tries on accents,
Acts.

All day, and they are at the lighthouse
The bird observatory
The ruined abbey.

One day you come across an old album, discover
A faded watercolor,
A poem that rhymes *horse*
With *gorse*.

A Woman in Wales

A woman in Wales
Shares a cottage by the sea.
Wind fills and luffs her hair like sails,

Dispatches clouds cross country,
Sending rain. In the sky, a light opens—
Then closes as if locked by latchkey.

Indoors, she puts away her notes, pad, and pens,
Fixes herself a cup of hot chocolate,
As women do in kitchens

Almost anywhere, but here, on a late
Afternoon in Wales,
The sea is as blank as if God would uncreate

Creation, no boats now or fishermen, only gales
Of steam climbing from her cup, a slick lacquer of cream
Cooling the chocolate, not even the mails

From the mainland running. Around here somewhere,
A newly abandoned dream, but what is a dream
But something that was never there?

The Spring

We went for walks but not together.

My footpath led me past meadow rue
Around a bend at the base of a hill
Where sprites were gathered, and there

I found a spring, almost invisible
But loud as a song
Three tenors might sing.

The water slipped over cool shale
Into a field where the children were having
A make-believe Bake Sale.

Tuppence for a mud pie, a shilling for a roll,
A bun's a farthing. Sir, are you on the dole?

I drowned a penny in spring water,
Wishing for a daughter.

Men Who Go to Work Each Day

And morning after morning they put on
The uniform of work—policemen, letter
Carriers, mechanics, waiters, well-built construction
Workers in yellow hard hats . . . do it whether
They wish to or not, these unknown men, with bosses
Who rule from nine to five like little tyrants
And add up everything in terms of losses
And think employees should be sycophants.
The teacher, the teller, even the NCO
Has someone over him, drawing a line
Somewhere, that he has always got to toe.
I think these men are sturdy, true and fine,
Arriving home at dusk to change their clothes,
Become the husbands and fathers everyone knows.

A Day Spent Walking and Writing

She stepped mindfully
Around the sheep dip,
The long slugs sliming
In dew, the snails.

Soon the sun was up,
And a fresh wind filled the sails
Of the boat, so far out it seemed to be miming
Progress rather than really

Making any, but she had covered miles,
And now the island was wholly
Dark, clouds worn thin as slippers.

Another day gone to pacing and rhyming.

The Manx Shearwater

On nights when there's no moon, the Manx shearwater
Will cry—almost a howl, a dog baying
At the moon, but no moon rises over water
And night is black beyond any mere graying.
Scientists study what these birds are saying;
The locals feel that it's a simple matter
Of socializing, of getting it on—and laying
Some eggs, of course—but the nightowl shearwater
Is mostly monogamous, and lives *en famille*
In nests that humans are not meant to see.
The shearwater is content with its own kind.
On nights when there's no moon, the Isle of Bardsey
Breaks its vow of silence, grows loud as a kennel,
As if nature itself were speaking its mind.

The Last Night

The girls are mopping the painted stone floor.
Papá has set his boots by the door.

He gives instructions; they obey.
There were thirty seals in the harbor today.

The girls are playing at Pop Singer,
But I have hurt my ring finger

By falling into prickly gorse.
Papá so likes a clean house!

The baby goats are black-and-white.
Perhaps I shall not sleep tonight

For there's no moon this time of month
Despite the prayers of our mad monk,

And nesting choughs and shearwaters
Will cry, as I for my lost daughters.

Learning to Live with Stone

A shore of washed stones
A sky the color of stone
A stone cliff

Stony face, stony heart

There is nothing here,
Twisted roots, sea taking the land
Back. Sea wrack
And rain.
                There is nothing
Here between us but stone.

One must learn to live with stone,
Make it a bed to lie on
A step to climb.

Carve.

What the Poet Wishes to Say

On Translation

Be warned, I tell my students.
A writer with nothing to write
is in danger of falling into
one or more of four
pitfalls: drink, drugs,
adultery, and translation.

Drink will sink you. Drugs
don't even deserve discussion.
Adultery is too expensive
for the young and when you are old
it is too exhausting.
This leaves translation.

Now, then. I'm sure you know
that every translation
is an interpretation
and that interpretation
displays a point of view,
which you must have. Get one.

To translate, you will need
a dictionary of the language
from which you are translating
and a dictionary of the language
into which you will translate.
Also, something to translate,

hereinafter referred to
as the text. Begin with a text
that is relatively easy:

short, clear, shapely.
Of course, "short, clear,
shapely" won't guarantee

a relatively easy text.
Take Catullus, the "Odi
et amo": merely two lines
but impossible to unpack
in English. It's been done
but never well enough.

Once you have your text
you'll want to do a word-
by-word translation, taking
note of what can be carried
into, say, English, and what
must be abandoned by

the roadside: the meter? the rhyme?
the lavender thyme spilling
over the stone wall in
Auvillar? You must,
sometimes, prune the text
to make room for imagery

that branches out from the *vocab-
ulaire* of the language, French, say,
that you are translating.
Okay. You know already
that Frost said poetry is
what gets lost in translation,

and so it is, standing
there helplessly, its arms
by its sides as cars zoom by

and the sun lowers itself
into the blue bath of
evening. But it would be true,

too, to say that poetry
may be found in translation.
The flowering branches grow
into new, dynamic forms,
inscribing themselves on air,
their blossoms bright as flares.

A new poem has grown
next to the other, yet not
as volunteer (far-flung,
defiantly independent),
but as a companion of
the heart of the other, two—

and maybe many more—
entwined and reflecting one
another in the blue
pond of the evening sky.
And yes, perhaps there'll be
anachronisms here

or there, but, really, so what?
You are not writing the work
for the time for which the author
wrote it. In fact, you are not
writing the work at all.
You are not Catullus, not

Sophocles, although, translating
Antigone, you felt
such sympathy for her

and her stupid uncle
you truly thought you'd be
torn in half, both halves

thrown to wolves, as were they,
in a sense, given that
the narrative thread of the play
is closer to a noose.
I've always loved that play
but it's one of those loves that hurt.

Be warned, I tell my students.
To translate, you must love
the text, and if you love
the text, you will be led
down blind alleys, through dark
parks, to the jumping-off

place where your sore need,
your ravenous desire
bind you to the book
you left on the stone wall
bursting with lavender thyme—
small blossoms thickly scented.

Love finds us out, even
the love of words. To translate
is to penetrate the text
until it yields, unfolding
meaning and music and swoons
beneath your ballpoint pen.

My students smile. They think
I'm being salacious, or modishly
ironic, but I'm not.

I want to teach them that
a pitfall is a pitfall
is a black oubliette

they'll not get out of unless
they know what they are doing.
A text merits respect
and must be handled with care,
you must recognize its allurements
and dangers. A dangerous text?

Oh yes, if it keeps you from
the work you meant to be
your own. Remember this,
dear students, as you kiss
or smoke in the rising tide
of ever-deepening night:

Translation adds to who
you are but takes away
your self. The question is,
Will you give your life
for someone else's work?

God help you now.

What the Poet Wishes to Say

What the poet wishes to say cannot be said,
in part because it has been said, and often,
before, but this was true when only the second
poet wrote. It becomes no truer with time.

The bigger reason the poet cannot say
what she wishes to say is that she wishes to say
something that seems to be a kind of music,
a word-field of music, as it's less a text
and more a space of time profoundly charged
by feeling, like the awe attendant to
our modest place among the huge events
of universal import: stars and novae,
the initiating burst of Many from
the One—the one what? Impacted point,
or god, or some computer-generated
simulacrum? In any case, the whole
of it.   If everyone could speak the whole,
then everyone would speak poetry, but
Molière's *gentilhomme* was perfectly pleased to learn
he had been speaking prose.
                              Even for those
whose language is poetry, the task requires
a life of: practice, contemplation, prayer.
(The latter two are sham without the first.)
This life begins in echo and extends
into apprenticeship, a period
that may be short or long but always ends,
if it ends, with the achievement of a vision
or "showing," as Julian of Norwich called her visions
of Jesus Christ, but we prefer "a view."

(Transported as we are by art and music,
the leap to faith remains a leap to faith.)
So say "a view," a world view if you must,
but know that you are only halfway home.
Even with the view. Even speaking poetry.
Because poetry is not the only language
you must master. You must also learn
the personal language that will convey your view,
and since your view, so similar to the ones
you love, also differs from them, if only
because the time in which you live and write
is different, you must invent that language,
hoping a few readers follow on the same
path and perhaps they will and perhaps they won't.
But how to make a language of your own?

In short, the process has to do with rhythm.
The racing rhymes of Dante's *terza rima*
so magnify the interlocking of
hell, earth, and heaven that the universe,
the medieval universe, becomes one verse.
And Chaucer's Wife of Bath is like a laugh
so full and deep it shakes the ground of England.
And Will, whose way with words created English,
creates as well the tense, or rueful, clash
between the life of action and the life
within the skull, that secret, teeming world.

Or consider a poet less removed
in time, whose reputation for that reason
is hard to know, yet Osip Mandelstam,
arrested and in exile, begging food
and blankets, honed the razor of his lines.
Discussing Osip, poet Joseph Brodsky
notes, "Whatever a work of art consists of,

it runs to the finale which makes for its form
and denies resurrection."
                        This is true
and not true, as it is, too, when he writes, "After
the last line of a poem, nothing follows
except literary criticism."
Both statements are rather more clever than correct.
What follows a poem is often a poem in response.
Or a poet may write a poem that enacts
its own resurrection.
                        As for the poet,
the poet aims not at immortality
of self or reputation but of what
he or she wishes to say, the world as it was,
or seemed to be, on that day in mid-October
when the hills were still green, the wildflowers
scattered like birdseed from a hand not seen
nor felt, and the various, changing, falling leaves
swirled up again, caught in a sudden updraft,
then settled on the ground like immigrants,
a huddling, a community of color.
A day when a small boy rushed to open the door
to shout "Bonjour, Madame!" to a woman whom
he'd never met and waked in her a feeling
of sheerest joy, salvific and abiding.
The poet wishes to say what life was like
here on the planet in the twenty-first
disturbing century and might, to do
so, think of her beloved Beethoven,
who, deaf and lonely, brought his art to such
sublimity, it is as if he wrote
his music among the spheres of music, working
at a desk of sky, the innumerable stars for lighting,
a gust of solar wind sending manuscript
flying. In the late piano sonatas,

you hear the composer placing his notes, solid
and silken as they somehow manage to be,
without hesitation but with deliberateness
exactly where they are supposed to go,
thereby fixing the apparatus of heaven
God had let fall idle.

The Life and Death of Poetry

If word came into world
Taking the form of man,
Poetry is body,
Flesh and blood we read,
A text that, like a heart,
Can move a heart to love.

The poem's heart must be cradled
Live in a loving hand.
Through vein and artery
The blood of it will bleed
As though to make a desert
Bloom, like brightened grove.

If angels flocked to herald
The birth of the one God-man,
They surely sang sweetly, clearly.
Did wise men following the lead
Of a star discover the art
Of reading the word from above?

And were there years untold,
The boy left alone
To play and think and try
His elders, who agreed
He might grow into the part
Of a good man who could move

God to pity his people?
Grown, he would teach God's plan
Even to the Pharisee.
So the poem, as yet unread,

Allowed to mature apart
From hectoring world, will give

Itself time to be called
Into the world, a fan
Of palm waving wildly
Where sandy roads fed
Into the main artery.
In the sky, a white dove

Cried, unconsoled
By the crowd shouting hosannas
To the man riding a donkey.
Someone scattered seed
Onto a low rampart
But the bird did not dive

For it, would not be fooled
By cajolery or praise or paean;
Even a dove has a duty
To fulfill, can fill a need,
Bemoan the human heart.
At the last stop, it hove

Into the doorway, furled
Its wings, and perching on
A ledge, with its beauty
Welcomed the one who'd heed
Its presence, its trembling heart,
The one who saw it hover

Through supper then tuck its bold
Head, for the night's duration,
Beneath a wing, mutely
Dreaming of birds once treed—

Here the bird startled—
By flood let loose to save

Believers, but what ship's hold
Rescued the child or man,
The woman, guilty only
Of praying river would recede,
Of loving rock and root
And green moss grown over

The flood-enriched land, gold
Under returning sun?
Why must the innocent die?
No God, and no church creed,
Tells us, and yet his feet
Were lovingly laved

By Magdalene, her gold
Whore's heart opened
To receive his respectful pity.
Trusting, willing to accede
To his requirements, heart beating,
She bowed her head and prayed,

And what did he behold
In that deferential woman?
A citizen of his city,
The kingdom of God. Indeed,
As she washed his aching feet,
He saw she longed to be saved,

To be freed and paroled
From her history of sin,
As did everybody
He met who was not dead
To himself, who knew the part
That each of us has played

In others' lives, how we killed
Their hopes, how cruel we've been
Accidentally and may still be,
The words we've left unsaid
And those wielded artlessly,
A blunt and shredding blade.

Do we believe in a stone rolled
Back, in a resurrected man?
We believe in poetry.
We believe language is the blood
Of the Lamb and the heart
Of the Heart we must revive

Again and again. Christ, cold
And sleepless on the mountain,
May have been an epiphany—
Or a blasted tree hooded
In fog rising out
Of nightwood and leaving

Like a ghost or, dark and coiled,
Like the shameful smoke of the ovens,
Or both. The poem must die
To the poet, it must be dead
To the poet's ego, go out
Of the poet's self, cleaving

To time's cross, stretched and nailed,
Forgotten, to be reborn
In the human heart,
The poem as mustard seed,
The poem as a work of art
That will gloriously live.

Or not. Perhaps the world
Pays no serious attention.

It does not matter. Poetry
Is not the human reed
Broken into many parts
On the turning wheel of life.

While autumn leaves are whirled
By wind and schoolchildren
Drop from the branch of a tree
That overhangs a raked bed,
A patchwork quilt of sorts,
With the laughter of those who thrive

In homes tenderly ruled
By loving parents, sun
Low in the deepening sky,
The kids' hands chapped and red,
While our planet cartwheels
Toward winter, we are alive

To hear the parents scolding,
The children racing in,
Their shouts falling to reverie,
To see the last sun spread
Against the sky like fine art
And day turn to evening.

Poetry's just poetry. The world
Is where what is human
Matters more. The body
Is as helpless as a reed,
But it has a heart
A poem can move to love.